The Christmas Jokes Game Book

For Kids

How To Play

Step 1

Split into two teams whether that be boys vs girls, kids vs parents, or any mix of your choice. If possible, also assign one person as a referee. You can also do 1 vs 1!

Step 2

Decide who gets to go first. Which team can do the most pushups? Which team can guess the number between 1 and 10 from someone not playing the game? Or just a good old fashioned rock paper scissors?

Step 3

The starting team has to tell a joke from the book. You can say the joke however you like and animate it too with funny faces, gestures, voices or whatever else!

Step 4

If everyone on the opposing team laughs, the other team gets a point! Set a limit for how many points it takes to win and the first team to reach the limit, wins!

What language does Santa speak?

North Polish

What do reindeer say before telling their best jokes?

This will sleigh you!

Who is a Christmas tree's favorite singer?

Spruce Springsteen

What's red and white and keeps falling down chimneys?

Santa Klutz

Where do Christmas plants go to become movie stars?

Holly-wood

How does a cow like to say Merry Christmas?

Moowy Christmas

How did Scrooge win the football game?

The ghost of Christmas passed!

What do snowmen call their kids?

Chill-dren

What did the peanut butter say to the grape during the holidays?

Tis' the season to be jelly!

Why did the apple pie start crying?

Because its peelings were hurt.

How do Christmas angels greet each other?

By saying, "Halo!"

What did the ghost say to Santa?

I'll have a boo Christmas without you!

What is the best Christmas present in the world?

A broken drum, you just can't beat it!

What do you call an old snowman?

Water

Where do snowmen go to dance?

A snow ball

What's a kid's favorite king during Christmas time?

A stoc-king.

What's Santa's dog's name?

Santa Paws

How many presents can Santa fit into an empty sack?

Only one because it's not empty after that!

What do you get when you cross Christmas and a duck?

Christmas quackers

What falls in the winter but never gets hurt?

Snow!

What is the ratio of a pumpkin's circumference to its diameter?

Pumpkin Pi

What's the key to a great Christmas dinner?

The turKEY

How can you make a turkey float?

You need 2 scoops of ice cream, root beer and some turkey!

Why can you never take a turkey to church?

Because of their fowl language!

What's everyone's favorite vegetable on Christmas?

Beets me.

What kind of bugs go oui oui buzz buzz on Christmas?

French Flies

What do monkeys sing at Christmas?

Jungle Bells

What is a cow's favorite holiday?

Moo Years Day

What do you call Santa when he stops moving?

Santa Pause

What happens when a Christmas tree gets a present?

He lights up!

What do chickens mail their Christmas cards in?

Henvelopes

How do snowmen get to work?

By icicle.

What sound does a limping turkey make?

Wobble, wobble

Why did Billy get low grades after Christmas?

Because everything gets marked down

during the holidays.

How many cranberries grow on a bush?

All of them.

Why do Prancer and Blitzen get so many coffee breaks?

Because they are Santa's star-bucks!

How do you greet a snowman?

By saying, "Chilly to meet you!"

What do you call a snowman with six pack abs?

The Abdominal Snowman

What goes oh oh oh ?

Santa walking backwards!

Why did Humpty Dumpty hate winter?

Because he had a great fall!

How do frogs open their Christmas presents?

Rippit rippit

Why did Santa plant 3 gardens?

So he could ho ho ho!

What kind of treat is never on time?

ChocoLATE

What did the turkey say to the PC?

Google, google

What do witches sing for Christmas?

Deck the halls with poison ivy! Fa la la la la la la la la!

What kind of photos do elves take?

Elfies

If fruit comes from a fruit tree, where does turkey come from?

A poul-tree

Why did the Christmas tree go to the barber?

He needed a trim.

What do you call raining turkeys?

Fowl weather

Why did the turkey cross the road twice?

To show he wasn't chicken!

What do snowmen eat for breakfast?

Frosted Flakes

When does Christmas come before Thanksgiving?

In the dictionary.

How does a snowman lose weight?

He waits for the weather to get

warmer!

Why does Santa work at the North Pole?

Because the penguins kicked him out

of the South!

If an athlete gets athlete's foot then what does an astronaut get?

Missile Toe

What did one snowman say to the other?

Do you smell carrots?

What does the gingerbread man put on his bed?

Cookie sheets

What does Santa say at the start of a race?

Ready, set, ho ho ho!

Why was the turkey on Comedy Central?

He was looking to get roasted!

What always comes at the end of December?

The letter R

What do you call a reindeer that wears ear muffs?

Anything you want! He can't hear you!

How does a sheep say Merry Christmas?

Fleece Navidad

What did the reindeer say to the football player?

Your Blitzen days are over!

What do road crews use at the North Pole?

Snow cones

What do snowmen like to do on the weekend?

Chill out.

Where do polar bears vote?

The North Poll

Why was the Christmas dinner so expensive?

It had 24 carrots.

What is a popular winter activity to do inside during the winter?

Snow and Tell

Why was the cook late to Thanksgiving dinner?

He lost track of thyme!

What are you giving Mom and Dad for Christmas?

A list of everything I want.

What do you get when you cross a Christmas tree with an Apple product?

A pine-apple

What did Santa say to Mrs.Clause?

It's going to rein-deer.

What do hip hop artists do on Christmas?

Unwrap

What did the hipster say the morning after Christmas?

I liked the turkey before it was cool.

What's the best thing to put into a pumpkin pie?

Your teeth

What's a pumpkin's favorite sport?

Squash

What do you call a turkey fumbling the ball in football?

A fowl play

Where does Santa stop for hot chocolate?

Star-bucks

What do reindeer hang on their Christmas trees?

Hornaments.

What did the mother turkey say to her disobedient children?

If you're father saw you right now,

he'd be rolling in his gravy!

What do you call a snowman that can walk?

Snow-mobile

What does a squirrel see on Christmas Day?

The Nutcracker

How do you get a turkey to fly internationally?

By getting a bird class ticket!

How is Drake like an elf?

He spends all his time wrapping!

What did baby corn say to mama corn?

Where's popcorn?

What do you call a shark that delivers toys on Christmas?

Santa Jaws

What sound does a turkey's phone make?

Wing wing

Where does Santa stay on vacations?

A ho ho ho-tel

Who delivers Christmas presents to dogs?

Santa Paws

What do you call Santa if he also lives at the South Pole?

Bipolar

What do you call the wrapping paper left over from opening presents?

The Christmess

What cars do elves drive?

Toy-otas

Who gives presents to cats on Christmas?

Santa Claws

What do you call buying a piano for the holidays?

Christmas Chopin

What do you learn at Santa's Helper School?

The elfabet

What is a turkey's favorite dessert?

Peach gobbler.

Why did the cranberries turn red?

Because they saw the turkey dressing.!

What did the turkey say to the turkey hunter?

Quack quack

What did the little elves have to do after school?

Gnomework

What do turkeys on space stations say?

Hubble hubble

What do you call it when you cut down a Christmas tree?

Christmas Chopping

What do you call a blind reindeer?

I have no eye deer!

What smells the most at a Christmas dinner?

Your nose

What do you call a sheep that doesn't like Christmas?

Baaaaaa humbug

What do you call Santa when he's smelly?

Farter Christmas

Where do turkeys go to dance?

The Butterball

What does a turkey drink from?

A gobble-t

Where does Santa keep all of his money?

In a snow bank.

What do you call a singing elf with sideburns?

Elfis

How did Darth Vader know what Luke got for Christmas?

He felt his presents.

What did Adam say to his wife on Christmas?

It's Christmas, Eve!

Why is it always cold during Christmas?

Because Christmas is in Decemburrrr.

What do you call Santa living at the South Pole?

A lost clause

What are Santa's little helpers called?

Subordinate clauses

What's your favorite Christmas food?

I know it's irrational but it's pi.

What do you get when you cross a snowman and a vampire?

Frostbite

What do you call people who are afraid of Santa?

Claustrophobic

What do you call an obnoxious reindeer?

Rude-olph

What does a turkey like to eat on Thanksgiving?

Nothing — it's already stuffed.

What do you call a cat on the beach at Christmas time?

Sandy Claws

What nationality is Santa Claus?

North Polish

Why does Santa Claus go down the chimney on Christmas Eve?

Because it soots him.

Why was Santa's little helper so sad?

Because he had low elf esteem!

What do you call a broke Santa?

Saint Nickel Less

Why shouldn't you pick a fight with Santa?

Because he has a black belt!

What is every parent's favorite Christmas carol?

Silent Night!

What's the name of Santa's detective brother?

Santa Clues

What do you call a greedy elf?

Elfish

What do fish sing during Christmas?

Christmas corals

What's the difference between Santa's reindeer and a knight?

One slays the dragon and the other's

draggin' the sleigh!

Merry Christmas!

Thank you for reading! We hope everyone enjoyed the book and had lots of fun.

As a special bonus, enjoy this exclusive preview of one our other popular titles!

Would You Rather

Book for Kids

A Hilariously Fun Activity Book

for the Entire Family

How to Play

Step 1

Split into two teams whether that be boys vs girls, kids vs parents, or any mix of your choice. If possible, also assign one person as a referee.

Step 2

Decide who gets to go first. Which team can do the most pushups? Which team can guess the number between 1 and 10 from someone not playing the game? Or just some good old fashioned rock paper scissors?

Step 3

The starting team has to ask a question from the book and the opposing team has 10 seconds to not only choose an option but to also give a meaningful reason as to why they chose what they did. The referee decides whether the answer is acceptable.

Step 4

The team can discuss their answer together but only one player can give the answer. The person answering has to alternate every turn.

Step 5

If the player who is answering can't choose or give a good reason then that player is out for the game and can't answer anymore or be involved in the team discussion.

Step 6

Repeat until all players are eliminated.

Step 7 (optional)

Decide whether it will be a single game or best of 3, 5 or 7.

Let's begin!

WOULD YOU RATHER...

Be a superhero

-OR-

a wizard?

Have the ability to fly

-OR-

read minds?

WOULD YOU RATHER...

Lick the floor

-OR-

lick **someone's** armpit?

Be a cat

-OR-

a dog?

WOULD YOU RATHER...

Fall into a puddle of mud

-OR-

a pile of yellow snow?

Do 100 pushups

-OR-

100 situps?

WOULD YOU RATHER...

Get yelled at by
Mom

-OR-

by Dad?

Run 10 miles

-OR-

bike 50 miles?

A Message From the Publisher

Hello! My name is Hayden and I am the owner of Hayden Fox Publishing, the publishing house that brought you this title.

My hope is that you enjoyed this book and had some fun and laughs on every page. If you did, please think about leaving a review for us on Amazon or wherever you purchased this book. It may only take a moment, but it really does mean the world for small businesses like mine.

Our mission is to create premium content for children that will help them build confidence, grow their imaginations, get away from screens, spend more quality time with family, and have lots of fun and laughs doing it. Without you, however, this would not be possible, so we sincerely thank you for your purchase and for supporting our company mission.

~ Hayden

Check out our other books!

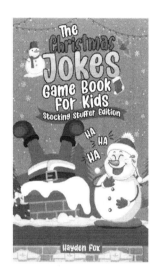

For more, visit our Amazon store at:
amazon.com/author/haydenfox